EMMA MICHELETTI

MASTERPIECES OF

PITTI

PALACE

TRANSLATED BY
PETER W. DENZER

BONECHI EDITORE - FIRENZE

VIA DEI RUSTICI, 5

Pitti Palace: *The courtyard*

PITTI PALACE

« And then Master Luca Pitti ordered Filippo to build for him outside of the gate of San Nicolò at Florence, in a place known as Ruciano, a rich and magnificent palace .... but greater in size than that already begun for him in Florence and raised to two floors ...., » so wrote Vasari. It was on August 1, 1461, that the Florentine Signory ceded to Luca Pitti, renowned and redoubtable gonfalonier of the Republic, a piece of land (now the site of the Boboli gardens) for the construction of a new, larger and more splendid dwelling.

Luca was virtually forced into the undertaking for the sake of « the large family with which he was blessed by the grace of God .... » The palace was begun according to the plans of Brunelleschi (died, 1446) and progressed to « the second floor with such size and magnificence that among Tuscan works there has not yet been seen one more rare or more magnificent .... » But then as swiftly as Luca Pitti's fame had come it

was to vanish. Driven by an inordinate love of power to join the plot against Piero de' Medici, son and heir of Cosimo the Elder, Luca was sent into exile when the conspiracy failed. Even the subsequent pardon by Piero, although it permitted him to return to the city, did not allow him to recover from his financial crisis. It was that, in part, and then his death in 1472, which forced Luca Pitti to abandon work on the palace which continues, however, to bear his name.

According to the ancient plans the palace was to have had a façade broadened by seven windows on its first floor and three great doors harmoniously spaced on the ground floor. A fresco by Vasari in the Palazzo Vecchio shows that the back of the palace was left unfinished.

In 1550 Eleanor of Toledo, wife of Cosimo dei Medici, first Grand Duke of Florence, acquired the palace for her family thus beginning a new and truly splendid period: « not long ago the illustrious Eleanor of Toledo, Duchess of Florence, on the advice of her illustrious consort, the Duke,

Pitti Palace – Monumental Apartments: *White room.*

bought the palace and spread out around it, partly on the level, partly on the height and partly on the slopes, a great garden filled with an array of all kinds of wild and domestic trees. There are to be found charming groves of an infinite variety of verdure that provide, in all seasons, a green cover for water, fountains, acqueducts, nurseries, bowers and hedges and an infinity of other things truly princely about which nothing can be said for the magnificence and beauty of the place must be seen to be believed. » Here it is Vasari who describes the birth of the Boboli gardens, the fantastic, bizarre and decorative work of Tribolo and Buontalenti.

It is always Vasari who provides the most faithful account, too, of the construction of the palace:

« .... since the plan of Filippo was not to be found His Excellence had the sculptor and excellent architect Bartolommeo Ammannati make another according to which work was begun and in large measure completed on the courtyard which is a rusticated work similar to the façade. ». Clearly, even at the distance of a century and in spite of changed taste, neither architect nor patron thought of departing from Brunelleschi's ideas. From 1558 to 1577 Ammannati worked on the courtyard which seemed to be by itself a true architectural masterpiece, especially for the far side which opens against the green slope of the hill. The architect found it necessary for practical reasons to close the two lateral doors opening in their place two large, grated windows. And so from the private palace of Luca Pitti grew the royal seat of the Medici. And within this splendid frame, there

Pitti Palace – Monumental Apartments: *Sala delle Nicchie.*

is a park rich with fantasy, with movement, with green. Here there is a spacious « classical » amphitheater, there are grandiose and pleasant fountains, paths arched over with the branches of ilex and laurel debouch into great avenues lined by dark cypress and stone statues. This frame of green, of water and of sculptured divinity is what the Florentines of old along with our contemporaries, with their innate sense of measure and thrift, refer to briefly as « the Boboli Gardens. » But the project is still far from complete. In 1620, Cosimo II of the Medici ordered to be carried into his sickroom the first stone intended for the new wings designed by Giulio Parigi who intended to add three windows to each side of the palace. Between 1640 and 1650 Ferdinand II commissioned Alfonso Parigi, son of Giulio, to enlarge the ground and first floors by adding five windows to each side and it was thus that the palace assumed its present aspect, lacking only the two wings and porches. The southern wing was completed under the direction of Giuseppe Ruggeri between 1764 and 1783 on a commission from the Lorraines who, in 1737, on the death of Gian Gastone dei Medici, the last of his line, became the rulers of Florence. The other wing carried forward under the direction of Gaspare Maria Paoletti until 1799 when Ferdinand III of Lorraine went into exile. After the restoration in 1815 the wing was completed by Pasquale Poccianti who, after the passing of the Grand Duchy, executed the noble entrance to the palace, a second monumental stairway and the direct passage from the interior of the palace to the Boboli Gardens.

From 1776 on it was Gaspare Maria Paoletti who carried forward the construction of the villa known as the Meridiana until it was taken over by Giuseppe Cacialli and then brought to completion by Poccianti while an enlargement of the east side of the palace was held in abeyance — it was that part destined to house the new collections of antique and modern art. The final embellishment of the structure was the entrance stairway to the Palatine Gallery executed in 1896 by the architect Luigi Del Moro.

The successive enlargements were executed with admirable fidelity to the original notions of Brunelleschi resulting as a consequence in a continual transformation of the interior so that today it is impossible to find among the labyrinth of large and small chambers, corridors, passageways and closets the original apartments that for half a century comprised the private dwelling of the Pittis. It was particularly the adaptation of the palace to the sumptuous needs of the grand ducal court that submerged the original layout of the interior. It is only approximately that we know where the Grand Dukes lived and which were the rooms of Violante and of Anna Maria Ludovica dei Medici. More vivid is the memory of the princes of the house of Savoy who held their court at the Pitti Palace during the five years from 1865 to 1870 when Florence was the capital of Italy.

Finally in 1919 Victor Emanuele III gave the palace to the state for public use and particularly to serve as a great museum. The Medici and the Lorraines furnished the rooms which today house

Pitti Palace – Monumental Appartments: *Throne room.*

the Palatine Gallery, the Silver Museum and the Monumental Apartments and which at one time were the apartments of Cosimo III, of Anna Maria Ludovica his daughter and Violante of Bavaria his daughter-in-law, of Prince Mathew and Crown Prince Ferdinand. The so-called *Room of the Stove* splendidly frescoed by Pietro da Cortona with representations of the Four Ages of Man (the artist's spendid drawings for these frescoes are kept at the Uffizi) and the Chapel still evoke a sense of the private lives of the Medici. Even in the time of Cosimo II and Ferdinand II there was some thought of bringing together the most important paintings and those most precious to the princes into a « private

gallery » that would extend through the living quarters and reception rooms of the palace. An antique inventory from the period of Cosimo III (1711-1725) shows the works to have been scattered from the « billiard » room to the « audience » chamber with still other pieces in rooms given the most curious names: the room of « the golden trinkets, » « the spur room, » and « the room of the dulcimers. » And to understand what might have been the taste of the Medici and Lorraines it is enough to remember that their collection included 11 works by Raffaello, 13 by Titian, eight by Tintoretto, 16 by Andrea del Sarto and 12 by Rubens. It was a Lorraine, Leopold II, the last of the family

Pitti Palace – Monumental Apartments: *Green Room.*

to rule Florence, who opened his private gallery to the public: « The sovereign clemency of Grand Duke Leopold II permits the lovers of art to visit the collection from nine in the morning to three in the afternoon of weekdays. » He may also have been responding to the pressure of new and more vivid cultural interests and above all to the profound social changes that came about as a consequence of the French Revolution and the Napoleonic era — Tuscany, too, had been deeply stirred.

On the ground flood of the palace are to be found the rooms of the Silver Museum established as they are now in 1919. Silver, gold, amber and Florentine mosaic work is housed in fine chambers that include a monumental room frescoed by order of Ferdinand II of the Medici to celebrate his marriage to Vittoria della Rovere. The fresco was executed by Giovanni da San Giovanni and after his death in 1636 by Francesco Furini, Cecco Bravo and Ottavio Vannini. The fabulous collection includes vases from the collection of Lorenzo il Magnifico engraved with his name, a lapis-lazuli service designed for Grand Duke Francesco I by Bernardo Buontalenti, vases of rock crystal, engraved cups fashioned by the goldsmiths of Ausburg chased with fantastic inventions, precious embroideries including the late fourteenth century altar cloth

from the main altar of Santa Maria Novella, perhaps the most beautiful of its period in Italy, still fresh and brightly colored. And then there are ivories, cameos and jewelry, most of it Renaissance, in gold, enamel and precious stones mounted with a bizarre and refined fantasy by the goldsmiths of France and Florence.

The Palatine Gallery is unique in Florence in that it maintains today its original aspect of a royal private collection of the highest quality. The collection is particularly rich in works of the 16th and 17th centuries and includes paintings by the most celebrated foreign and Italian artists set in stupendous richly carved and gilded frames. Ceilings and walls are sumptuously decorated — there are frescoes which, depicting myths and classical triumphs, are veiled allusions to the glory of the Medicis. Pietro da Cortona who, as already noted, executed the frescoes in the Room of the Stove from 1637 to 1640, was later commissioned to fresco the rooms named after Venus, Apollo and Saturn. The ceilings are richly populated, full of movement and light. Once the work was under way Pietro da Cortona left to his student Ciro Ferri (who worked from 1659-1665) the task of completing the frescoes in the Apollo and Saturn chambers. In the 17th century Bernardino Poccetti, known as « il Volter-

Pitti Palace – Monumental Apartments: *Bathroom.*

8

Palatine Gallery: Room of the Stove – *Frescoes by Pietro da Cortona. In the photo above, the frescoes depicting the Golden Age and the Silver Age; in the photo at right, the fresco depicting the Iron Age.*

rano », gave his name to a room in which he frescoed scenes from Florence and Sienna and some allegorical figures which represent the virtues of Vittoria della Rovere. Then in the 19th century, continuing the tradition of his predecessors, Ferdinand III of Lorraine commissioned Luigi Sabatelli to fresco the room then known as « dei Novissimi, » but renamed, from the frescoes themselves, the saloon of the Iliad. Sabatelli's work was continued by Pietro Benvenuti, Luigi Ademollo, Bezzuoli and Collignon.

This was how the Palatine Gallery evolved into a singular, splendid complex, the only gallery of its kind where beauty is surrounded by beauty and where architecture, fresco and painting are joined into an indissoluble and interdependent unity. And then all around there is the green serenity of the Boboli Gardens, the bright gushing of the fountains, the play of light and shadow in Buontalenti's courtyard and the vast space of the piazza giving from each of the many windows a fresh and luminous prospect that completes the beauty of every room.

From the Palatine Gallery we pass into the Monumental Apartments, formerly the reception rooms for the Grand Dukes and then for the King of Italy .Only Umberto and Margherita actually lived here and their rooms are still preserved. These quarters have also undergone various transformations and their 17th and 18th century aspect preserve the feeling of the Napoleonic and post-imperial epochs. Only the « Sala di Bona » with its frescoes by Poccetti retains its original aspect but the other rooms, sumptuously furnished with precious materials, furniture and above all priceless tapestries, recall vividly a vanished world of luxury and royalty where delicate Chinoiserie harmonizes with the jewel-like splendor of Florentine mosaic, mirrors, neo-classic statuary and the great chandeliers of the White Room and the « Sala delle Nicchia. »

Venus Room

PETER PAUL RUBENS (1577-1640)
1 – *Ulysses on the Island of the Pheaci.*
2 – *The Peasants Return from the Fields.*

Rubens was born in Siegen, Westphalia, and studied art under Flemish masters but his taste and spirit were much influenced by the great tradition of 16th century Italian painting and especially Caravaggio, Carracci and Titian. Rubens thoroughly assimilated his Italian influences which were well joined with his altogether Flemish exuberance, love of life and painting technique. Form and color dominate his work lending it at times a serene tranquillity and at other times a vigorous movement and dramatic sensibility.

Ulysses on the Island of the Pheaci gave the Flemish master an excuse to display his rich virtuousity. It was painted, with the aid of students, in 1634. *The Return from the Fields,* painted about 1637, is certainly one of the most glorious landscapes to have been painted up until that time.

1

2

SALVATOR ROSA (1615-1673)

1 – *Seascape.*
2 – *Seascape.*

Savator Rosa, Neapolitan by birth and temperament, is one of the most complex personalities of the Italian 17th century. He was a painter, poet, philosopher, musician and a member of literary and artistic academies. Brilliant of intellect and lively of spirit, he was of such diverse talents as to give rise to legends.

A pupil of Luca Giordano, Rosa rebelled against the pompous and sumptuous Neapolitan Baroque painting without turning to the antisocial realism of Caravaggio or Bamboccianti. In his painting, which for the most part was concerned with the themes of the day, he expressed a lively interest in reality without abandoning grandiose landscapes and bloody battles although his work remained typically rich in 17th century fantasy and capricious Baroque. His learning was enlivened by vibrant colors and a facile brush. In some of his work there is a veiled satire which explodes violently in the inscriptions.

1

TITIAN (1485-1576)

1 – *The Concert.*
2 – *Vincenzo Mosti.*
3 – *The Beautiful Woman.*
4 – *The Englishman.*

After beginning his career as a painter under the direction of Giovanni Bellini, Titian soon turned fascinated to the great art of Giorgione who created the particular Venetian tonality. He followed Giorgione not only in his painting but also in his wide culture and it was not long before he succeed him as the foremost 16th century Venetian painter. He transformed the sweetly human and lyrical art of his master into a stronger and more virile monumentality, into an intense drama that he expressed particularly in a rich gamut of colors, tones and textures laid on with decidedly heroic brushwork.

And if his vision of the world is vast, illuminated by violent flashes of light that enlarge the luminous atmosphere, it may be that he is responding to distant echoes from the grandiose art of Michelangelo. During the entire passage of his long life he continued to assimilate new experiences, enriching his art and repeatedly renewing its youth up until the most tormented work of his old age.

The works in the Palatine Gallery are all of his youth or early maturity. The first, chronologically, is *The Concert,* once perhaps identified as a painting by Giorgione, acquired by Cardinal Leopold

2   3

dei Medici in 1654 from the collection of Palo del Sera. Now the work is almost unanimously attributed to Titian. Only he could have obtained such thick coloring full of an intense, immediate luminousness and the delicate exchange of sentiments and glances particularly in the ravished ecstasy of that is musically intense and soft as the emanations the player while every tone develops with a delicacy of passionate souls.

The Portrait of Vincenzo Mosti can be dated about 1520. It was also an acquisition of Cardinal Leopold and is one of the most beautiful of that period with its harmonious blending of brown and white tints and the delicate flesh of the sensitive face. Then, perhaps around 1536, he produced a representative masterpiece, *The Beauty,* which comes from the Urbino collection of the Della Rovere family.

This is a splendid study of budding feminine beauty, an open chubby face and solid youthful flesh magnificently set off by the blue end violet of the elegant clothing. The light diffused over the subject gives a unified value to the masterfully treated forms and rich colors. The portrait of a gentleman, known as *The Englishman,* comes from a later period, almost at the close of this middle maturity about 1545« It is also part of the Della Rovere inheritance having belonged to Vittoria, wife of Grand Duke Ferdinand II dei· Medici and the last of her line. For a long time the painting was thought to be the portrait of˙Howard, Duke of Norfolk and then it was identified as the jurist Ippolito Riminaldi. The portrait is fascinating for the perfect equilibrium of all its movements, colors, composition, setting, for that hazy, greenish light that is suffused over the background, for that delicate softness of flesh but above all for the intensity of the expression which gives brilliant vitality to the great soul which is perhaps that of Titian himself, creator of the work.

Apollo Room

ANDREA DEL SARTO (1486-1530)
Sacred Family.

The art of Andrea del Sarto is informed by the last of the 15th century Florentines but he was also able to absorb the grandiose plasticity of Michelangelo blending and softening it with the toning taught by da Vinci while he turned to Fra' Bartolommeo for a monumentality of structure. From Raffaello he learned to give his work a sweet serenity. Perhaps his style was a bit eclectic but a strong sense of balance and an altogether Tuscan restraint permitted him to overcome much awkwardness so that while none of his work reaches the level of genius, a rich and noble production caused Vasari to refer to him as « a painter without faults. » Certainly few other painters were as capable as he in the use of such an exalted artistic language for the interpretation of so many facets of his time.

The Sacred Family executed, according to Vasari, around 1529 for Ottaviano dei Medici is from the latter part of his life and undoubtedly reflects a moment when Michelangelo was dominant in his memory. Here there is a drammatic tension expressed in the attitude of Saint Elizabeth and the whirling agitation of the Child stretched out against the foreground. Andrea's style softens in the thoughtfulness of the young Madonna whose face is lit with a soft light. The warm harmonies of shading reveal the influence of Raffaello in the distance while an intense tonality seems to be of Venetian origin.

GUIDO RENI (1575-1642)
Cleopatra.

Reni's work is so discontinuous and varied in style that he is difficult to classify. Here, at one point, he follows Raffaello in the representation of pure beauty or at another point he is Venetian in his taste for an intense coloration or he will turn to a striking realism reminiscent of Caravaggio or he will even indulge in the courtly academicism that is associated with Carracci. Thus he passes from a refined intellectualism to a throbbing, almost amorous realism most apparent in some splendid portraits and wherever he chooses to extend the full gamut of his palette.

Cleopatra was given to Cardinal Leopold in 1640 by the Marquis Cospi of Bologna and can be dated around 1639. In its entirety the work perhaps derives from Carracci. It is strongly melodrammatic but enchanting in its range of colors, a silvery harmony that touches on violet or a tenuous gilt tonality when a clear light falls on a basket of figs.

Mars Room

BARTOLOMÈ MURILLO (1616-1682)
Madonna with Child.

This painter from Seville is part of the great tradition of Ribera and the young Seville masters Zurbaran and Velasquez. He attempted, perhaps in vain, to model himself more directly after the fashion of Italian art but never realized his ambition to travel in Italy. At one time he was a painter of great realism but his best work tends toward elegance, soft coloring, softly melting, perhaps under the influence of Van Dyck. The grace of a smile, the soft folds of a cloak, a blond curl, all give life to a new picture even tending to repeat in his sacred subjects. The Virgin and Child, the origin of which remains unknown, reveals a bond with Van Dyck in composition, the forthright tonality and the freedom from *chiaroscuro* complexities. Murillo is still under the influence of the 16th century but the great dark eyes of Mary, her well modelled face framed in dark hair shows how dear to Murillo was this type of gypsy Virgin.

ANTONIO VAN DICK (1599-1641)
Portrait of Cardinal Guido Bentivoglio (see page 22).

Van Dyck was Rubens' greatest student and certainly one of his most valued collaborators. In 1622, having been launched on his career by the master and carrying his recommendations, he set out for Italy to study its masterpieces, especially those of Venice. Genoa became his favorite residence and there he became a popular portraitist preferred above all by the aristocracy. He has left us a rich and accurate testimony of his genius in a numerous series of important portraits. What is most striking is an immediate perception of certain human aspects of his subject, a worldly elegance in his style and the infinite lightness of his brush. The Portrait of Cardinal Bentivoglio is one of the most beautiful executed by the painter and since Bentivoglio was made cardinal in 1621 the painting, which belonged to Grand Duke Ferdinando III, must be dated after that year. The luxurious setting, richly rendered, underlines the aristocracy of the subject.

PETER PAUL RUBENS (1577-1640)
The Four Philosophers.

The Four Philosophers which is datable from 1614 to 1615 shows the painter in a more studious and humanistic aspect. This painting is a portrait of the painter, his brother Philip, Giusto Lipsio and Jan van de Wouwere. Here a chromatic subtlety dominates and creates a luminousness that serves to ennoble the subjects. This Flemish painter is unable to avoid faithful attention to details of the real world which he reveals in the precious rug, the silky gleam of the black clothing, the dog stretching out toward his master and especially in the delicate coloring of the tulips in the window, the simple homage to the bust of Seneca.

Jupiter Room

PERUGINO (1466-1523)
Madonna of the Sack.

Even the first works of Perugino permit us to see how he developed under the influence of the great art of Piero della Francesca to be able to interpret with a particular delicacy softly luminous backgrounds of landscapes bathed in the gentlest light.

In Florence around 1470 he most certainly frequented Verrocchio's busy workshop which was a formative center for a whole generation of artists. But always, even when his art became tired, monotonous and often repetitious there shone in his work the clear atmosphere of Piero, a throbbing vitality which he then left as an inheritance to Raffaello, his greatest pupil.

This work takes its name from the sack on which the Infant is seated. It was part of the collection of Cardinal Leopold dei Medici unless we are to recognize its earlier origin. Critics are not agreed whether this is entirely the work of Perugino but to him certainly are due the idea, the composition and the serene landscape in the background, so sweetly and truly Umbrian, almost lost in an infinity of impalpable luminousness. Mary is certainly the work of his hand. Her face is very similar to those in the paintings of Cambio di Perugia who followed faithfully the truest and most deeply felt expressions of his master. In the absorbed and sweet face there is a play of light and shadow so sensitive that at times it seems to have been informed by the shading of da Vinci.

VENETIAN SCHOOL OF THE 16TH CENTURY
The Three Ages of Man.

The painting comes from the inheritance of the Crown Prince Ferdinand.

The anonymous work is one of the best known of the Palatine Gallery and at various times has been attributed to the most celebrated authors including Lorenzo Lotto, Morto da Feltre, Giovanni Bellini, and Giorgione. The last is the most convincing because of the felicitous agreements of rather low tones enriched by an almost palpable atmospheric light. There is also the rather romantic dreaminess of the three figures lost in a subdued complaint of a more or less recent past or vague imaginings of an uncertain future.

In its entirety there is still something of the measured composition of the 15th century but there is a forecast, too, particularly in the coloration, of the freedom and exuberant display of the 16th century.

BRONZINO (1503-1572)
Guidobaldo della Rovere (see page 26).

A generation younger than the great Tuscan mannerists Pontormo and Rosso Fiorentino, Bronzino developed with a vigorous clarity but his more poetic temperament led him away from the sometimes cerebral intellectualism of the mannerists. He transformed the often complex structural composition of Pontormo into simpler and more linear schemes. The fame of Bronzino rests solidly on a series of famous portraits of the highest Florentine and Italian society and the painter himself was bound in a particular fashion to the Medici family. As a portraitist he is more free from the grandiose influence of Michelangelo and the cerebrality of Pontormo.

The portrait of Guidobaldo della Rovere became part of the Medici collection with the transferral of the inheritance of Vittoria dei Medici. It was probably painted at Pesaro between 1530 and 1538 when the prince was about 18 years old, according to the inscription.

The refined art of Bronzino is evidence by the aristocratic aspect of the youth whose breastplate is burnished and gilded, whose entire costume displays an infinite richness of detail. All the almost regal pomp of this portrait is heightened by the controlled light tones which tend to increase the detachment of the young man. In contrast there is the lively, throbbing affection of the dog which stretches out to receive the caress of his master.

PETER PAUL RUBENS (1577-1640)
The Sacred Family.

The Sacred Family is from the collection of Cosimo III dei Medici and can be dated 1616. It is a delicate picture of the serene family life of the painter himself and is a tribute to his affection for his wife and children who are interpreted with a happy creativity that exploits the full range of Rubens' brilliant pallette and his exquisite rendering of flesh tones .

Jupiter room: *table inlaid.*

FRA' BARTOLOMEO (1472-1517)
Deposition.

Influenced by the preaching of Savonarola he became a Domenican friar and at first attempted a synthesis of the new 16th century art modes current in Florence and then demonstrating in the intensity of his coloring an awareness of Venetian art. His style was open and spacious on the order of Michelangelo's but sweetened by the shading of da Vinci which in his hands, however, became almost a smokey shadow, his colors singing with a vivid tonality.

The Pietà, now at the Pitti, comes from the convent of San Gallo where it remained until 1529 when the Augustinians, fearing a siege of Florence, abandoned their residence. The painting then went to the church of the Pretoni in via San Gallo whence it passed to S. Jacopo tra i Fossi and finally it was taken into the Medici collection. It is one of the most beautiful and deeply felt works of the painter. The drama of the subject matter is purified in the delicate profile of Mary as she lightly caresses the head of her Son and in the intense sadness of Saint Joseph who sustains the pallid, delicate body that almost throbs with a mother of pearl light. But Madelaine seems to want all this tragedy for herself as she embraces with despair the legs while the red of her gown gleams in harmonious contrast with the luminous white of Mary's veil.

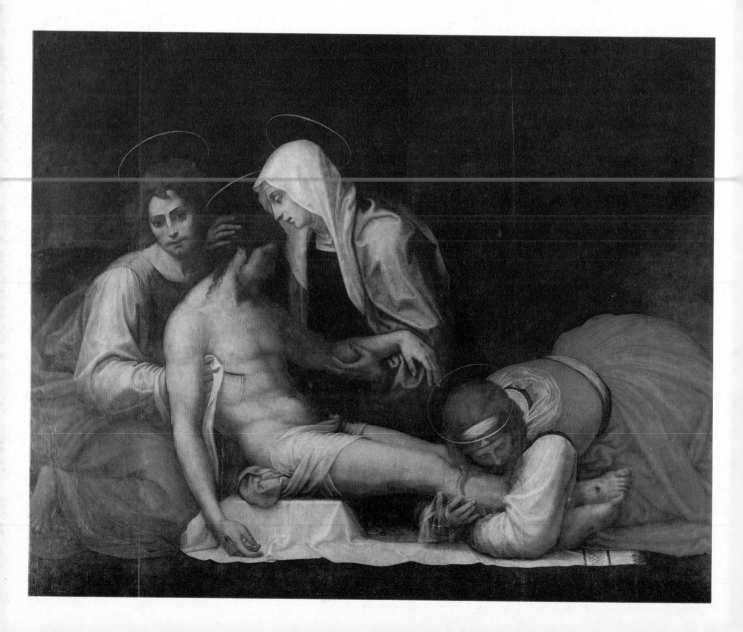

Saturn Room

RAPHAEL (1483-1520)
1 – *The Veiled Woman.*
2 – *Madonna of the Chair.*
3 – *The Vision of Ezekiel.*
4 – *Madonna of the Grand Duke.*
5 – *Portrait of a Pregnant Woman.*

Urbino, the city of Raffaello's birth, was bathed in the irradiations of Renaissance art emanating from Florence and from childhood Raffaello was under this influence expressed at the Montefeltro court by Paolo Uccello, Piero della Francesca, Sandro Botticelli and Laurano who was the architect for the splendid ducal palace. But the grace of Umbria was within both Raffaello and Perugino his master so that it was only at Florence that he was to enlarge the horizons of both his visual and emotional worlds looking to da Vinci for his shading and to Fra' Bartolommeo for his first orientation toward the Venetian palette. An then there was a long stay in Rome which opened the serene mon-

umental world of Bramante, chief architect of Saint Peter's. In Rome he also encountered the dramatically powerful and dynamic forms of Michelangelo who is indicated by tradition as Raffaello's rival. All his instruction and all influences he absorbed and made his own in a serene and balanced art of vast horizons and supreme beauty.

The Madonna of the Chair can be dated between 1515 and 1516 and was already part of the Medici collection shortly after the death of Raffaello. In 1589 it was exhibited in the Tribune of the Uffizi and from 1700 it has been in the Palatine. Raffaello returns here to a more vivid immediacy of feeling

2

and expression in the Mother's embrace of her Son, in the sweet, imploring gesture of San Giovannino. The composition is completely knowledgeable and forms almost a dynamic circle in which, responding to a vague impulse, Mary's knee is raised. At the same time the painter abandons himself to a most happy gamut of colors from red to green, to blue, to yellow.

The same chromatic splendor is to be found in *The Veiled Woman* where there is an almost Baroque movement of rich materials that enfold the flowering beauty of the young woman who tradition indicates as the Roman mistress of the painter. She is turned three-quarters in a confident, almost monumental spacial setting. The painter's attention lingers on the beautiful face, the folds in the sleeve, on the play of light on satin and velvet, on the necklace of agate and amber.

The small but grandiose *Vision of Ezekiel* is perhaps Raffaello's most lyrical expression in this blazing triumph of light and clouds which together with the powerful vision of the Almighty soaring among angels in the sky, surrounded by the symbols of the Evangelists annihilates any other possibility for the origins and nature of man. Ezekiel, too, is in ecstasy, overwhelmed by the superhuman power of God.

RAPHAEL (1483-1520)

The Madonna of the Grand Duke, acquired by Ferdinand III of Lorraine in 1799 is from his Florentine period, the year 1506, the year of the Madonnas. The da Vinci-like tones became a light shading which enveloped the forms and faces in a subtle veil rendering them more sweet, soft and luminous.

Iliad Room

Lorenzo Bartolini: *Charity.*

RAPHAEL (1483-1520)

The same shading is to be found in the female portrait known as *The Pregnant Woman* diffused over the slightly faded face. The shadowing emphasizes the planes, the expression and gives vibrancy to the red of the sleeves, the orange of the jacket, the black and white highlights of the skirt and hairdressing.

GIUSTO SUSTERMANS (1597-1681)

1 – *Prince Mattias de' Medici* (see page 37).
2 – *Valdemaro Cristiano, Prince of Denmark* (see page 38).

Fleming from Antwerp, Sustermans retained always his rich color sense which he inherited not only from Rubens but also from Van Dyck and Franz Pourbus. His style, however, remained his own, particularly in the use of fiery, almost bloody colors, livid shadows and finally an excessive resort to white lead. He dedicated himself particularly to portraits seeking, like a good Fleming, a noble interpretation of his subjects who were dressed in regal clothing or in knightly battle dress showing their royal lineage. A good deal of his artistic life was spent at Florence where he remained from 1620 to his death, as a painter and portraitist attached to the court of the Medici.

Prince Mattias dei Medici, the last son of Grand Duke Cosimo II, was above all a warrior and in this portrait described by Baldinucci as « a lively portrait of Prince Mattias as valuable as any other from his brush, » the painter is moving with his subject toward the happy peak of a Baroque period.

The other portrait, identified as that of the Prince Valdemaro Cristiano of Denmark, is perhaps a finer work almost as if the painter is competing with Rubens, Van Dyck and Cornelio de Vos in producing a delicate picture of youth with an appropriate restraint of color and shade.

DIEGO VELASQUEZ (1599-1660)
Portrait of Philip IV of Spain on Horseback (see page 39).

Diego Velasquez, « painter to the king, » was a painter from childhood. Student of Francisco Pocheco of Seville he went to Madrid where he achieved court recognition becoming not only a painter to the king but his close friend as well. His series of court paintings made him famous. Two trips to Italy in 1629 and 1649 put him in touch with great Italian art, especially Venetian painting, the strong coloring of which impressed him.

Lordly, established, sure of himself, his art followed a grand curve of evolution providing a superb lesson in painting that began with his first realistic work and went on to his aristocratic, elegant and profound work of full maturity.

This work at the Pitti, by some held to be an old copy by Juan Batiste del Mazo, Velasquez' son-in-law, was ,according to Baldinucci, sent to Florence where it was to serve as a model for Ferdinando Tacca who had been commissioned to execute a bronze equestrian statue of the king. The colors are vivid and luminous, clearly deriving from the Venetians but beyond any doubt put to canvas with the particular taste and skill of Velasquez who provided the inspiration for so much 19th century painting and perhaps, even modern painting .

1

2

SODOMA (1477-1545)
San Sebastiano.

Sodoma, born at Vercelli, was the youngest of the group of Lombard pupils of Leonardo da Vinci but his art flourished mainly at Siena which he chose as his home and where he lived until his death with the exception of brief periods at Monte Oliveto Maggiore, Rome, Florence, Lucca and Pisa. After Leonardo, Raffaello influenced most his lively and facile talent. His lively transformation of the others' artistic experiences into pleasing forms, a rich production and an extravagant and vivacious character made him popular in Siena where his painting style came to be truly dominant.

San Sebastion was painted for the Company of San Sebastian in Camollia at Siena and was commissioned in 1525. Vasari said of it: « rare painting, truly beautiful and worthy of praise. » It was a processional standard and therefore was painted on both sides. It remained in Siena until 1786 when it was acquired for the grandducal collection at the Uffizi. It came to the Palatine in 1928. It is properly considered one of Sodoma's masterpieces and partakes of that rather sensual, morbid and religious sentimentality such as would captivate a people as passionate as the Senese. A rather Nordic taste tends to prevail, as always, in the landscapes Sodoma illuminated in the background with sudden lights and spectral shadows.

Room of the Education of Jupiter

ÇARAVAGGIO (1573-1610)
Sleeping Cupid.

Caravaggio, moved by the strong realism of the Lombards Savoldo, Moretto and Moroni, set out to combat the courtly academicism of Carracci with a heroic fidelity to truth and at Rome, more than anywhere, produced that impressive painting which by the use of intense shadow and brilliant saber blows of light represents sacred scenes as literally true, actually lived. Sometimes Caravaggio's subjects are serene but usually they are involved in intense drama and suffering.

On the back of this canvas of a sleeping Cupid — once the property of Cardinal Leopold dei Medici — is inscribed « Maresi (Merisi) da Caravaggio, in Malta, 1600. » This means that it is one of the works of the last years of the painter who was in Malta in 1608, two years before his death. The painting is consistent with his taste for dark shadows which accentuate, where they are interrupted by sudden lights, every fullness of form. Light and shade make this sleeping child seem solid and heavy as sculpture. And still the painter refuses to take his subject out of a strongly realistic setting even to make a creature of pure beauty.

CRISTOFANO ALLORI (1577-1621) *Judith.*

Cristofano Allori was the first pupil of his father Alessandro who, in turn, was the foster son and student of Bronzino. Cristofano preferred the eclectic tastes of Bolognese art circles and in his time was highly esteemed in Florence for the delicacy of his drawing and the warm blendings he achieved with his colors.

He led an irregular life and permitted himself to be ruined by a woman — known as la Mazzafirra — he immortalized in one of the most beautiful paintings of 17th century Florence. This is the Judith of the Pitti collection. According to Baldinucci the head of Holofernes is a self portrait while the servant girl is a portrait of his mistress' mother. Without doubt the painting as a whole is strongly reminiscent of Caravaggio especially in the sensitive rendering of fabrics and the crude horror of the severed head. But the painting is dominated by a vivid color sense, by softly iridescent yellows, reds and whites and brilliant highlights in the velvets and damasks. Nor does the artist neglect the physical beauty of the softly gentle faces and poses that still evoke the classical. All this emphasizes again how the Florentine art world remained closed to the more profound and violent problems and temptations of Caravaggio.

RAPHAEL (1483-1520)
Madonna of the Window Pane.

The Madonna of the Window Pane was produced during the first years of Raffaello's stay in Rome and was perhaps painted for Bindo Altoviti. Vasari records the painting as already the property of the Medici, placed by them in the chapel of the Palazzo Vecchio. The hand of the master, already confident with rich experience, it to be recognized in the attitude of affectionate tenderness of the women around the Child more than in the rather mannered stylization of the Virgin and San Giovannino and the expansive composition illuminated by a white light which is, however, warm and diffused by white lines from the window which gives its name to the painting.

FILIPPINO LIPPI (1457-1504)
The Death of Lucretia.

Something of the great art of Botticelli is re-captured in the delicate work of Filippino Lippi, son of Filippo. He translates the vibrant feeling of Botticelli into a more tranquil and lighter form accentuating the melancholic with sometimes an idyllic touch, at others more strongly felt and always against a background of melting languor.

The work has already been attributed to Sandro Botticelli but then Berenson put forth the name of a hypothetical « friend of Sandro, » who was easily identifiable as Filippino Lippi. The work was executed around 1480 on a panel which may have been the facing of a large chest. The tragic story of the Roman lady provoked feelings consistent with the sentiments of those who were familiar with death. The theme is almost contradicted by the serene calm of a setting among Albertine buildings closed within a space prolonged by either luminous walls or open solemn arches through which glow bright sky and slender bushes. Brilliant areas of violent light render the colors, in general of great refinement, more vivid until they are almost lost in the profound black of the great portal.

Prometheus Room

BALDASSARRE PERUZZI (1481-1536)
Apollo and the Muses.

Baldassarre Peruzzi, born at Siena but active above all in Rome where he became part of the circle of Raphael, is better known as an architect than as a painter. His masterpieces, in fact, are the Farnesina and the Palazzo Massimo alle Colonne, both of which buildings are in Rome. Of decidedly Mannerist tendencies, Peruzzi creates delicately pictoric effects even in his architecture, where he unites allusions to nature with a luminous, vibrant impression. Again, when he takes up the brush, as in this small panel, Peruzzi takes his inspiration directly from ancient Roman painting, with its harmonious movements and delicate chromatic gradations.

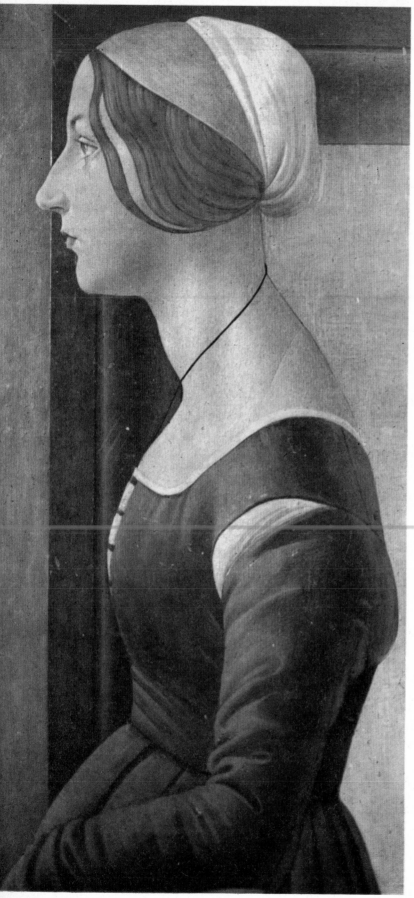

SANDRO BOTTICELLI (1445-1510)
The Beautiful Simonetta.

Botticelli transformed the dynamic tension of Antonio Pollaiolo into a musical rythm and in his most mature and splendid period became the poetic interpreter of literary and philosophic myths that exalted the perfection and intelligence of man. In his portraits and in those sacred and pagan paintings his art evidenced itself as a hymn to beauty in which a slight melancholy was expressed, a quality of the ineffable. It was only at the end of his life that a more profound introspection appeared in his work shutting him off from the brilliant light that at Florence was beginning to illuminate the name and work of Leonardo da Vinci. This closed spirit seems to be his ultimate style above all in the drawings for *The Divine Comedy*, deftly executed but forming an enormous poetic communication with the world and thought of Dante. This delicate portrait has already been identified as one of « two beautiful female heads, in profile, of which one was said to have been the mistress of Giuliano de' Medici, » cited by Vasari in 1568 « in the wardrobe of his highness Duke Cosimo. » Thus by tradition and in the most ancient inventories it came to be known as « Simonetta Vespucci. »

But there has been some discussion as to the identity of the young woman in the portrait just as the attribution of the painting has been debated. Perhaps she is Fioretta Gorini, who was also loved by Giuliano de' Medici, and mother of the then future Pontiff Clement VII. And notwithstanding authoritative opinion to the contrary the painting is the work of Botticelli's hand. There is clear and certain testimony in the line that draws a precise profile against a measured architecture that establishes a dynamic vividness of a Botticelli style in the period still close to the influence of Pollaiolo. There is a tranquil and poetic agreement between the calm, unified coloring and the gracious quiet of the gentle young woman.

GUIDO RENI (1575-1642)
Young Bacchus.

It is the same light that illuminates a cup of wine in the *Young Bacchus* and falls on an enamelled vase. This work from Reni's early period is datable between 1615 and 1620 and belonged to the Crown Prince Ferdinand. At that moment Reni had just become aware of the work of Caravaggio and had taken from him only the art of making objects tangible. There is none of the human drama and the strong contrasts of light common to the great Lombard. All, instead, is peace and calm, harmonious rythms and refined color.

PONTORMO (1494-1555)
The Martyrdom of the Eleven Thousand.

Without doubt Pontormo is the leading figure of the style known as Florentine mannerism. He was a young pupil of Leonardo da Vinci and then of Piero di Cosimo but his most important collaboration was with Andrea del Sarto then under the influence of Michelangelo. But he was soon to add to the monumentality of his master an intense vibration, a secret restlessness that shines in glances, reflects from movements and colors sometimes stridently. Then the vibration developes into a increasingly violent tension, dramatically passionate in thought and form of which the plastic expression is more refined, more fleeting and even a little bitter in the tormentedness of certain profiles and in the serpentine winding of limbs and clothing while colors flame now with sudden lights and then fade into a most original tonality of a crystalline purity.

« The eleven thousand martyrs condemned to death by Diocletian and crucified in a forest « was a work executed, » according to Vasari, « for the women of the hospital of the Innocents » and then passing to the ownership of Vincenzo Borghini. Wherever there is any possibility for movement it is always exploited and dramatized. Da Vinci's studious attention to the shape and substance of man is unified here with Michelangelo's tragic awareness of suffering. But the fantasy of Pontormo transforms every element into a desperate and dazzling caprice at times reaching toward a frenzied cry of despair as if the painter was unable to find a solution to a continually agonizing problem. The colors are subtle, applied in a delicate tonality to forms drawn with an unfailing confidence that is altogether Florentine.

FILIPPO LIPPI (1406 about-1469)
Madonna with Child.

Lippi early joined the Carmelite family at the monastery in Florence and his first work was strongly influenced by Masaccio. He took active part in the first Florentine re-birth transforming the heroic style of Masaccio into a warm and happy art far removed from the pious mysticism of Angelico.

This work was probably executed for Leonardo Bartolini around 1452 in the period of the frescoes at the Cathedral in Prato.

It may be that the private patronage under which Lippi often worked influenced his style. This round painting at the Pitti seems to confirm this hypothesis. Here the painter lingers on the beauty and elegance of the Virgin revealing his pleasure with soft coloration that sometimes brightens with an unusual tonality now shaded around the borders

or now reinforced in sudden, new reflections. Here again Lippi confronts the problems of composing within the round but does not seek to coordinate the figure in the foreground with that lively but distant little activity in the background. There is a happy alternation of open space with volume and the depths are heightened by geometrically designed paving. The shape of the circle is not determining — the same composition would remain unchanged in another format, square or rectangular. There is an infinity of poetry in the scene of the Nativity of Mary, in the elegant movements of the women, in the offering up to the mother of the luminous Infant, in the coyness of the child hiding behind the mother dressed in a violent red. And above all in the delicate distraction of the gentle Virgin lost in her distant thoughts while she offers to the Child a shining pomegranate.

Room of Justice

PAOLO VERONESE (1528-1588) *The Baptism of Christ.*

Veronese was the last of the 16th century Venetian geniuses. Inheritor of a mannerist culture he soon opened his soul to the classic forms then in vogue in Venice, forms based above all on color and the illusions of a rational linear perspective. He looked naturally to Titian but his mind was open to other experience and he never forgot the great atmospheric openness of the painters of the school of Parma — from Correggio to Parmigianino. For his opulent figures of young women triumphant in their beauty there are often backgrounds and frames, open sky of the most limpid blue and great white and airy architecture. He was also a notable portraitist, attentive to the spirit of his subjects. He set his noble men and women among luxurious silks, velvets and furs. The Baptism of Christ, came from Ancona in 1688 and it is not among the most significant works of the painter but the alternation of spaces and masses gives it life and movement. The decorative sense is strong and the subject matter stands forth brilliantly in clear light and luminous colors.

Flora Room

ANDREA DEL SARTO (1486-1530)
The Life of Joseph.

The Life of Joseph was executed « to decorate a room » in the house of Pier Francesco Borgherini and the work remained in that house until 1584 when it was acquired by Francesco I de' Medici. In each of the two scenes are represented a number of events in the life of Joseph with a full sequence of uninterrupted continuity. The work, executed around 1511, permitted Andrea to solve problems of movement, of light and color either in open air or against a background of an ample, fantastic but solidly constructed architecture. The work is developed with a great deal of freedom, with a contrapuntal alternation of volumes and shapes in a happy interplay of tensions while a vivid fantasy brightens even more vivid colors that light points of reference to bring the attention to the reality of people and objects.

Room of the Cherubs

GODFRIED SCHALKEN (1643-1706)
Girl with candle.

Schalken's painting is pleasant and while he can be placed in the school of Utrecht he has obviously been inspired by the magic light of Gherardo delle Lotti. He also shows the influence of Caravaggio but the severe realism of the latter has been transformed by being centered gracefully on the happier aspects of daily life in the country.

This little work, rather well known, is signed and comes from the Medici Villa at Poggio a Caiano where it remained until 1773 when it went to the Uffizi and then in 1928 to the Palatine. Particularly delicate is the play of light on the smiling face and on the hand which, screening the candle, assumes a rosy transparency.

RACHELE RUYSCH (1664-1750)
Flowers.

Rachele Ruysch, pupil of Van Aelst, belongs to one of the lesser Dutch schools of the 17th and early 18th century. This school was concerned with the precise rendering of nature, the faithful portrayal of fruit and animals, objects bathed in a clear, limpid light that perfectly defined forms.

We can see in this painting, acquired in 1825 by the Grand Duke Ferdinand III of Lorraine, all the artist's fascination with the precise details of delicate flowers, soft, crystalline fruit, nests of sparkling little eggs, butterflies, darting lizzards, caterpillars, and bees. In the sudden light that glows on each object everything moves and throbs under the delicate but precise brush of the artist.

Poccetti Gallery

DOMENICO FETI (1588-1623)
The Lost Coin.

After his preparation in Tuscany, in particular under the tutelage of Cigoli, he was irresistably drawn to Caravaggio. The instruction in such realism and human truth remained valid for him all his life even when he achieved a taste for more intense colors learned from Rubens whose soft, luminous brushwork Feti brought to his post as court painter to the Duke of Mantova. There is generally a light, sweet vein of melancholy in his sacred scenes and feminine portraits while in the small works, such as this one at the Pitti, he demonstrates a fresh and spontaneous sense of immediate reality. The painting, inspired by the evangelist parable, comes from the inheritance of Cardinal Leopold and is a work fresh and spontaneous. Everything the painter registers here is set down with precision and a balanced sense of values. There is the shabby furnishing of the room, the girl anxiously searching for her little lost treasure, the almost magic light radiating from the little lantern reflects in minor tones highlights reminiscent of Caravaggio's.

Room of the Allegories

Emilio Zocchi: *Michelangiolino*.

IL VOLTERRANO (1611-1689)
Parson Arlotto's Joke.

He was a student of Matteo Rosselli but was much drawn to the clear atmospheric openness of Pietro Cortona and the still earlier Correggio. The sparkling liveliness of his style is gained from Giovanni da S. Giovanni while the gentle graces of Bernardino Poccetti inspired him toward an expression compounded of limpid light and clear color almost like fresco.

His masterpiece in *Parson Arlotto's Joke,* a portrait of the witty parish priest of San Cresci, subject of rich and lively anecdotes of typical Floren-tine flavor. The work is recorded by Baldinucci as « ... a bizarre painting of the renowned barrel joke played by Arlotto to confuse the shrewd land-lord .... » In 1693 the painting was among the fur-nishings of Prince Ferdinand at his villa in Poggio a Caiano.

This luminous, animated painting attributed for a long time to Giovanni da S. Giovanni, was restored to Volterrano by the critics. It reveals the artist's interest in the lively popular wit of his times.

Aurora Room

L'EMPOLI (1551-1640)
Still Life.

His was the conservative somewhat anachronistic world of 17th century Tuscany. Faithful to the most traditional forms of painting l'Empoli was particularly inspired by the art of Andrea del Sarto.

More than in his sacred pictures however balanced and dignified they may have been he achieved his greatest success in still lives and his kitchen scenes.

This painting, like others, was acquired by the Florentine galleries in 1923 and is rich in plastic qualities, its forms outlined by a steady light which in places contrasts with the profound shadows of a background delicately suggested.

In this work the painter demonstrates all his mastery in a multiplication of planes, in the creation of forms suggested with an incredible perfection of drawing.

For him, truly, the still life — the portrayal of chickens, ducks, cabbages or lemons, pieces of meat and ham — was an opportunity to display the virtuosity of genius.

Room of the Drums   Hercules Room

1

SILVER MUSEUM

1 **Silver Museum** – Agostino Mitelli: Room I.

2 **Silver Museum** – Room IV.

3 **Silver Museum** – Jasper vase.

4 **Silver Museum** – Bernardo Buontalenti: lapis-lazuli vase.

2 3 4

Silver Museum – Cup of Diana di Poitiers.

2   **Silver Museum** – Ottavio Vannini: Lorenzo among the artists of his time.

INDEX